MACMILLAN READERS

PRE-INTERMEDIATE LEVEL

WILLIAM SHAKESPEARE

Romeo and Juliet

Retold by Rachel Bladon

MACMILLAN READERS

PRE-INTERMEDIATE LEVEL

Founding Editor: John Milne

The Macmillan Readers provide a choice of enjoyable reading materials for learners of English. The series is published at six levels – Starter, Beginner, Elementary, Pre-intermediate, Intermediate and Upper.

Level control
Information, structure and vocabulary are controlled to suit the students' ability at each level.

The number of words at each level:

Starter	about 300 basic words
Beginner	about 600 basic words
Elementary	about 1100 basic words
Pre-intermediate	about 1400 basic words
Intermediate	about 1600 basic words
Upper	about 2200 basic words

Vocabulary
Some difficult words and phr
understanding the sto
story and
lev

Contents

A Note About The Author

William Shakespeare is believed to be the greatest English writer of all time. He was born in Stratford-upon-Avon, in England, in April 1564. His father was a wealthy merchant – he bought and sold wool and leather. In December 1582, Shakespeare married Anne Hathaway, the daughter of a farmer, and they had three children. We know very little about Shakespeare's early life. Some people believe that he worked as a teacher. Other people think that he became a member of a travelling group of actors. But we do know that by 1592, Shakespeare was living in London. By then, he had already become quite well-known as an actor and a playwright[1].

At that time, in the early 1590s, the first theatres were just opening in England. In 1593, these new theatres and their actors had a difficult year. The theatres were often closed because of the plague – a disease which killed many people. But the following year, Shakespeare joined a new group of actors called The Lord Chamberlain's Men, and they became very successful. In 1598, they built their own theatre, The Globe, which was unusual because it had a round shape. Theatres at that time were very different to the modern theatres of today. There was no scenery and no curtain, and there were no intervals[2] or breaks between scenes. Women were not allowed to act, so they were played by boys. Most of the theatres did not have roofs, so plays were only shown in good weather and in daylight.

In 1603, Queen Elizabeth died, and James I became the King of England. King James liked Shakespeare's work very much, so he asked Shakespeare's group of actors to work for him. After that, they were called the King's Men, and they often performed[3] plays for the king. In about 1607, Shakespeare stopped acting. After that time he lived mostly in Stratford. He had become very wealthy, and was a very important person in Stratford. He died there on his birthday, in 1616.

Shakespeare wrote about 37 plays, including *A Midsummer Night's Dream*, *Romeo and Juliet*, *Hamlet* and *Macbeth*. He also wrote many beautiful poems. Many of Shakespeare's plays were only published as books after his death. In Shakespeare's time, people used to write plays very quickly. The actors performed them a few times and then they threw them away. No one really thought of keeping plays for people to read. Because of this, the plays of Shakespeare that we read today are probably not exactly the same as the ones that he first wrote.

Shakespeare used many different styles of writing in his plays. He was very clever at writing beautiful poetry, and he could use words to make pictures of things in people's minds. His plays showed very clearly what was going on in the world, and the people in them always seemed very real. Because of this, Shakespeare's plays are still performed all over the world today, and people in schools, colleges and universities have been studying his work for many years.

A Note About This Play

Romeo and Juliet is a very famous play about two young people who fall in love with each other. They both come from very important and wealthy families. However, their families, the Montagues and the Capulets, had an argument many years before. The play is about how Romeo and Juliet continue to love each other although their families are enemies.

The story of *Romeo and Juliet* takes place in the north of Italy. The Montague and Capulet families both live in the city of Verona, and most of the play happens in Verona. However, in one scene Romeo is in Mantua, a nearby city. The events that happen in the play take place over just four or five days. This makes the emotions of the play feel especially strong.

Shakespeare wrote many tragedies – very sad plays in which people die – and *Romeo and Juliet* is one of these. The play is about the difficulty of being idealistic – believing in something which is good but very difficult to make happen – in the real world. The love between Romeo and Juliet is very strong, but it is also impossible because of the argument between their families. The play is very famous because it has such an interesting but sad story, and such beautiful love poetry.

Romeo and Juliet was probably written and performed for the first time in 1595. We cannot be sure of the exact year. The story of the lovers was already quite well-known in England before Shakespeare wrote his play. This was because there were several other plays about Romeo and Juliet at that time. There were also other versions of the story, and a poem called *The Tragical Historie of Romeo and Juliet*, by Arthur

Brooke. Shakespeare followed this poem closely when he wrote his play. As well as using the story, he used many of Brooke's characters. Some of the lines and speeches are even very like ones from Brooke's poem.

Shakespeare's *Romeo and Juliet* was first published in 1597. However, the 1597 edition of the play was not actually written by Shakespeare. It was probably put together from the actors' lines, and from what people wrote down or remembered about the play. The second edition of the play, published in 1599, was actually written by Shakespeare.

This Reader is a short and simple version of *Romeo and Juliet* for students of English. Therefore, some of the things that happen and some of the things that people say in Shakespeare's play have been taken out. Because of this, Scenes 4 and 5 in Act 1, and Scenes 1 and 2 in Act 2 have been put together in this version. Act 3, Scene 4 and Act 4, Scene 4 have also been taken out completely. Finally, Act 5, Scene 3 is a little different in this version. In Shakespeare's *Romeo and Juliet*, Paris comes to the Capulets' tomb[4], and fights with Romeo, who kills him. But in this Reader, Paris does not appear in Act 5, Scene 3.

There are also several characters from Shakespeare's play who do not appear in this version. They are servants from the Capulet and Montague families, musicians who arrive to play at Juliet's wedding, and the apothecary[5] who Romeo goes to see.

7

This Version of Romeo and Juliet

This Macmillan Reader includes some 'real' extracts of text from *Romeo and Juliet*. We hope that these texts will help the students to both understand, and enjoy, Shakespeare in the original. The extracts follow immediately after their simplified form. They are shaded in grey and have a separate glossary. In the glossary, words that are old English (no longer used in today's English) appear in *italics*. See the example (from pages 25–26) below:

Juliet: The only man I have ever loved is from the only family I have ever hated! I fell in love with him without knowing who he is. And now it is too late. Oh, what a way to fall in love for the first time!

Juliet: *My only love sprung from my only hate.*
Too early seen unknown, and known too late.
Prodigious birth of love it is to me
That I must love a loathed enemy.

simplified text

sprung from = come from
prodigious = very great
loathed = hated

original text

glossary

The People in This Story

The Capulet Family

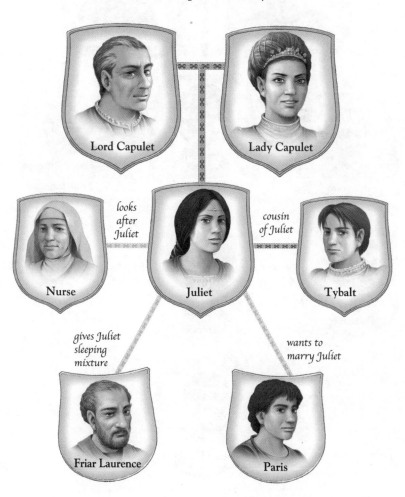

Lord Capulet

Lady Capulet

looks after Juliet

cousin of Juliet

Nurse

Juliet

Tybalt

gives Juliet sleeping mixture

wants to marry Juliet

Friar Laurence

Paris

The Montague Family

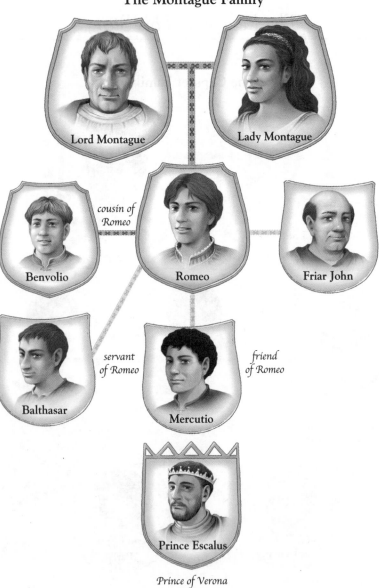

Lord Montague

Lady Montague

Benvolio

cousin of Romeo

Romeo

Friar John

Balthasar

servant of Romeo

Mercutio

friend of Romeo

Prince Escalus

Prince of Verona

Act 1, Scene 1

[Verona, Italy. Servants[6] of the Montague and Capulet families are fighting in the street. Benvolio, holding his sword[7], is trying to stop them fighting. Enter Tybalt]

Tybalt: So you're fighting with the servants now, are you, Benvolio? *[Pulls his sword out]* Come and fight with me, and let me kill you!

Benvolio: I don't want to fight with you. I am just trying to stop these men fighting. Put your sword away! Or use it to help me keep the peace.

Tybalt: How can you talk about peace when you are holding your sword? Peace! I hate that word. I hate it as much as I hate all the Montagues – and you! *[Stabs[8] at Benvolio with his sword]* Here, take that!

[Some old men from the town arrive with their swords to try and stop the fighting. Enter Old Capulet and Lady Capulet, wearing their night clothes]

Capulet: What's all this noise about? *[Sees Tybalt and Benvolio fighting and stands forward] [to his servants]* Bring me my sword!

Lady Capulet: *[Holding him back]* No! You are too old to fight!

Capulet: *[Pulls himself away from Lady Capulet]* There's old Montague! He is holding his sword. Why should I stand back when he is ready to fight? *[to his servants]* Bring me my sword, I said!

[Enter Old Montague and Lady Montague]

Montague: You villain[9], Capulet! *[to his wife, who is trying to hold him back]* Don't hold on to me! Let me go!

Lady Montague: No! You'll stay right here!

11

[Enter Prince Escalus with his attendants[10]]

Prince Escalus: *[Shouting above the noise of the fighting]* Listen to me, you enemies[11] of the peace! What a terrible thing to fight with your neighbours! *[No one hears the Prince and the fighting continues]* You there! *[Shouting more loudly]* You men, you animals! Can you only put out the fire of your anger with blood? Put your swords down, and listen to your angry prince, or I will punish[12] you all. *[The men finally hear the Prince and stop fighting. The Prince turns angrily to Capulet and Montague]*

This is the third time that people have fought in the streets because of your silly arguments. You have broken the peace of our town three times. *[Points to the old men from the town]* Look at these people! They are old men. They haven't picked up their swords for years, and now they have had to use them again to stop you fighting! If you ever cause trouble in our town again, I will punish you by death. Capulet, come with me now. Montague, come and see me this afternoon. Everyone else can go.

[Exit all except Montague, Lady Montague and Benvolio]

Lady Montague: I'm so glad that Romeo wasn't here fighting. Have you seen him today, Benvolio?

Benvolio: Yes, madam[13], I have. I couldn't sleep last night, so I went out for a walk just before dawn[14]. I was walking among some trees on the other side of the city when I saw Romeo. I went to talk to him, but as soon as he saw me he hid himself away in the wood. I wanted to be alone myself, and I realized that he probably did too. So I didn't follow him.

Montague: *[Sighing[15]]* He has spent many mornings in that wood. His tears have made the morning's dew[16] even wetter, and his sighs have added more clouds to the sky. But as soon as the sun comes up, he quietly sets off home, heavy with sadness. He hides himself away in his room, covers the windows, and shuts out the daylight. He is turning his days into nights! I am very worried about him.

Benvolio: Do you know why he is so unhappy, Uncle?

Montague: No, I don't know what the problem is.

Benvolio: Have you asked him?

Montague: Yes, I have spoken to him. And a lot of our friends have tried to speak to him, too. But he won't talk about it. He has completely closed up. He is like a bud[17] that is being eaten by a worm[18]. He cannot open his sweet leaves

13

up to the air or show his beauty to the sun. If only we knew why he was so unhappy, we could try to help him.

[Enter Romeo]

Benvolio: *[Seeing Romeo]* Here he comes. Leave me alone with him. I'll try and find out what is wrong.

Montague: Well, I hope you have better luck than everyone else. *[to Lady Montague]* Come, madam, let's go.

[Exit Montague and Lady Montague]

Benvolio: *[to Romeo]* Good morning, cousin.

Romeo: It isn't still the morning, is it?

Benvolio: It is just nine o'clock.

Romeo: Oh, when you are sad, time goes so slowly. Was that my father who hurried away just now?

Benvolio: Yes, it was. But why does time go so slowly for you? Why are you so sad? *[Romeo says nothing]* Are you in love?

Romeo: In love but . . . *[Stops]*

Benvolio: In love but what?

Romeo: In love with someone who has no love for me.

Benvolio: Oh, poor Romeo. Love looks so gentle, but it can feel so cruel[19] and hard.

Romeo: And although love cannot see, it still finds the people it wants. *[Suddenly sees where the men have been fighting]* Oh, there's been a fight! What was that all about? *[Benvolio starts to speak but Romeo stops him]* No, don't tell me. I can guess. The Capulets were fighting the Montagues. This trouble was caused by hate. But love is causing more trouble in my heart than hate has caused here. I am in love with someone who doesn't love me. It is like fire that is cold, or sleep that keeps you awake. *[Turns to go]* Goodbye, my cousin.

Benvolio: *[Quickly turns to follow Romeo]* Wait for me, Romeo. Let me come with you.

Romeo: With me? This isn't me, Benvolio. I have lost myself. I don't know where Romeo is.

Benvolio: Tell me. Who is it that you love?

Romeo: I love . . . a woman.

Benvolio: Yes? *[Waits for Romeo to continue]*

Romeo: A woman who will not let love near her. She will not listen to sweet talk, or let people look at her with love.

Benvolio: Do you mean that she has taken a vow[20] of chastity[20]?

Romeo: Yes, she has. Oh, what a waste! *[He is quiet for a moment]* Her name is Rosaline. She is so beautiful and so intelligent . . . but I can never have her. It is so unfair! She has promised never to love and that promise has turned me into a dead man.

Benvolio: In my opinion, you should forget about her.

Romeo: How can I forget about her? Show me how.

Benvolio: You need to look at other beautiful women.

Romeo: That will only remind me that Rosaline is more beautiful. *[Turns to go once more]* Goodbye, Benvolio. You can't teach me to forget her!

Benvolio: But I will – I promise that I will.

[Exit Romeo and Benvolio]

Act 1, Scene 2

[In the street near the Capulets' house. Enter Capulet, Paris and one of Capulet's servants. Capulet and Paris are talking.]

Capulet: . . . So Montague and I will be punished if we don't keep the peace. We are so old, I don't think that should be too difficult for us!

Paris: You are both such honourable[21] men. It is sad that you have had this argument for so long. *[After a moment]* But my lord[22], I told you a while ago that I would like to marry your daughter, Juliet. Have you thought any more about that?

Capulet: I'm afraid that my answer is still the same. Juliet is too young, Paris. She is not even fourteen yet. Perhaps in another two years she will be ready to marry.

Paris: There are many women younger than her who marry and become mothers.

Capulet: Yes, and I believe that marrying so young can damage[23] them. My daughter is my only child. She is my hope for the future. Try and win her love first, gentle Paris. If she wants to marry you then I shall agree. I'm having a big party here tonight. We have invited a lot of people, and you should come too. There will be some very pretty young girls here. Come along and meet them all. Then you can decide whether my daughter is really the one you want. Come with me now. *[to his servant, giving him a list]* Go round the city and find the people on this list. Tell them that they are invited to my house this evening.

[Exit Capulet and Paris]

Servant: 'Go and find the people on this list!' *[Looks at the list, turning it around, but obviously can't read the names]* Well, that's like asking someone to catch fish with a pencil! I can't read, so how can I find the people on this list? I'll have to look for someone who can read.

[Enter Benvolio and Romeo, talking]

Benvolio: Come on, Romeo. You need to fall in love with somebody else. A new fire stops an old fire burning. A new pain stops you worrying about an old one. Fall in love with someone else, and your old love will die.

Romeo: *[Scornfully²⁴]* Oh yes! And put a banana leaf on your cut leg, and it will feel fine! *[Sees Capulet's servant]* Good evening, good man.

Servant: Good evening, sir. Can you read, sir?

Romeo: Yes, I can read my unhappy future in my sadness.

Servant: *[Confused]* But can you read words, sir?

Romeo: Yes, I can read. *[He takes the list the servant is holding and reads it out]*

Martino and his wife and daughters;

Lord Anselm and his beautiful sisters;

Placentio and his lovely nieces;

Mercutio and his brother Valentine;

My uncle Capulet, his wife and his daughters;

My beautiful nieces Rosaline *[Romeo sighs]* and Livia;

Valentio and Tybalt;

Lucio and Helena.

That sounds like an interesting group of people. Where are they all going?

Servant: To my master's²⁵ house. He is the great rich Capulet. Come and have a glass of wine with us – as long as you are not a Montague. Good day, sir.

[Exit Servant]

Benvolio: Rosaline, who you love so much, will be at this

17

party at Capulet's house. And all the most beautiful women in Verona will be there too. Let's go along. I shall show you other women and you can compare them with Rosaline. I'll make you see that she is not as beautiful as you think.

Benvolio: *At this same ancient feast of Capulet's*
Sups the fair Rosaline, whom thou so loves,
With all the admired beauties of Verona.
Go thither and with unattainted eye
Compare her face with some that I shall show
And I will make thee think thy swan a crow.

ancient = very old (Capulet has been having parties like this for a long time)
feast = a large party with lots of food and drink
sups = eats
fair = beautiful
thou = you (subject)
admired (admire = to look at something that you think is beautiful)
thither = there
unattainted = clean, fresh
thee = you (object)
thy = your
swan = a beautiful white bird with a long neck
crow = a large ugly black bird

Romeo: I will come to the party. But not because I want to see other women. I will come to see my beautiful Rosaline.
[Exit Romeo and Benvolio]

Act 1, Scene 3

[At the Capulets' house. Enter Lady Capulet and Nurse]

Lady Capulet: Nurse, where's my daughter? Bring her here, please.

Nurse: *[Calling]* Lamb! Juliet! Where are you?

[Enter Juliet]

Juliet: What is it, Nurse?

Nurse: Your mother has come to see you.

Juliet: *[Turning to Lady Capulet]* Here I am, Mother.

Lady Capulet: I want to talk to you about something. Nurse, you know that Juliet is nearly fourteen now.

Nurse: Goodness me, yes, that's right. She will be fourteen in two weeks. Oh, and it seems like only yesterday that she was a little girl. *[Thinks about something and smiles]* I remember, when she was about three, she fell and cut her head. And my husband picked her up and said, 'Did you fall on your face? You'll remember to fall on your bottom next time, won't you, Juliet?' And do you know what? The pretty little thing stopped crying and said 'Yes'. *[Nurse laughs]*

Oh, I shall never forget that! It was so funny. She just stopped crying and said 'Yes'. *[Nurse laughs and laughs as she remembers the story]* Oh, you were the prettiest baby I've ever looked after. If I could see you get married one day, it would make me very happy.

Lady Capulet: Well, that's just what I wanted to talk about. Tell me, Juliet, how do you feel about getting married?

Juliet: I haven't thought about it at all, Mother.

Lady Capulet: Well, you need to think about it now. There are many younger ladies than you here in Verona who are mothers already. When I was your age, you had already been born. And I've come to tell you that Count Paris, who is a fine young man, would like to marry you.

Nurse: *[Very excited]* Oh, Juliet, young lady! Count Paris – what a perfect man!

Lady Capulet: *[Smiling]* He is a very handsome young man.

Nurse: Oh, yes, he's a flower! He's a perfect flower!

Lady Capulet: Do you think you can love him, Juliet? You will see him tonight at the party. Read his face like a book. If there is anything you cannot find there, look in his eyes. Every book needs a cover, and every handsome man needs a beautiful wife. Then the book can be locked shut, full of love. Juliet, when you marry someone, you share everything they have, without losing anything yourself.

Nurse: No, you don't lose anything – you grow bigger. *[Laughs]* Especially when you have a baby!

Lady Capulet: What do you think, Juliet? Do you like the idea of Paris's love?

Juliet: I'm sure that I will like the idea when I see him. But I shall only do what you want me to do, Mother.

[Enter a servant]

Servant: Madam, the guests have arrived and dinner is ready! Everyone is looking for you, and asking for Miss Juliet. Please come with me.

Lady Capulet: We're coming. Juliet, Paris is waiting for you.

Nurse: *[Excited]* Go on, girl! Have a lovely time!

Act 1, Scene 4

[At the Capulets' house. Enter Romeo, Mercutio and Benvolio with some other men, who are wearing masks²⁶. Some of them are carrying torches.²⁷]

Romeo: Let me carry a torch. I don't want to dance. I am heavy with sadness, so I shall carry a light.

Mercutio: No, gentle Romeo. You must dance.

Romeo: Not me. You are all wearing your dancing shoes. But my heart is so heavy, it pulls me to the ground and I cannot move.

Mercutio: [to one of the other men] Give me a mask! [The man gives him an ugly mask and Mercutio puts it on, laughing] An ugly mask for an ugly face!

Benvolio: Come on, let's knock and go in. We are late already.

Romeo: [to himself] I have a terrible feeling that something will happen tonight. Something will begin at this party, and it will bring my useless life to an early death. But there is nothing I can do about it. [Turns to his friends] Come on, then, gentlemen.

[They walk around the stage]

[Enter Capulet, Lady Capulet, Juliet, Tybalt and Nurse with all the guests. They welcome Romeo and his friends, who are all wearing masks]

Capulet: Welcome, gentlemen. I'm sure the ladies will all want to dance with you. Oh, I remember the days when I wore a mask to parties and could whisper things in a pretty lady's ear. But not anymore. Not anymore! Anyway, you are welcome, gentlemen. Let's have music! Clear the floor! And dance, girls!

21

4/2/02/82

[Music plays and they dance]

Romeo: *[to a servant, pointing at Juliet]* Who is that lady dancing with the man over there?

Servant: I don't know, sir.

Romeo: *[to himself]* Oh, she could teach the torches how to burn brightly. She shines like a jewel[28] in the night – her beauty is too precious[29] for this earth. Next to the other women, she looks like a snowy dove[30] in a group of crows[31]. When the dance is over, I shall watch where she stands. If I could touch her hand . . . Did I think that I was in love before? Forget about that! For I am seeing true beauty for the first time now.

Tybalt: *[Hearing Romeo's voice]* This man sounds like a Montague. *[to his servant boy]* Bring me my sword, boy. *[Exit servant boy]* *[Angrily]* How dare[32] he come here, wearing a mask, to scorn our celebrations? I will kill him for this!

Capulet: *[Hearing Tybalt]* What's the matter, Tybalt? What are you so angry about?

Tybalt: *[Pointing at Romeo]* Uncle, that man is a Montague, our enemy. The villain has come here to scorn our celebrations.

Capulet: *[Looking at Romeo in his mask and suddenly recognizing him]* Oh, it's young Romeo, is it?

Tybalt: Yes, it's that villain Romeo!

Capulet: Calm down, Tybalt. Leave him alone. He seems like a very polite gentleman. In fact, I have heard from other people that he is a good young man, and very well-behaved. I would never be rude to him in my own house. So leave him alone. Do what I say. Don't look so angry.

Tybalt: It is the only way to look when one of the guests is a ▮ I won't allow it.

22

Capulet: [*Whispering angrily*] Whose house is this, mine or yours? Do what I say! 'I won't allow it!' Who do you think you are? You're going to start a fight among my guests, are you? You're going to tell everyone what to do?

Tybalt: We should do something, Uncle.

Capulet: Oh, should we? You are a childish boy! You want to go against me, do you! You are a very rude young man. Now go quietly and be polite. [*Loudly, to the dancers, as the dance finishes*] Very good, my friends!

Tybalt: I shall leave Romeo alone. But I am afraid that there will be terrible problems because he has come here tonight.

[*Exit Tybalt*]

Romeo: [*Standing next to Juliet, taking her hand, and whispering quietly in her ear*] I know I should not touch your hand. It is too perfect for my rough touch. But my lips are ready to smooth away that touch with a gentle kiss.

Juliet: Good sir, you are unkind to your hand. After all, people touch the hands of holy[33] statues[34]. It is like a holy kiss.

Romeo: Do holy statues have lips?

Juliet: Yes, they do. And they use their lips to pray.

Romeo: Oh then, holy statue, let our lips do what hands do. Let me kiss you.

Juliet: Holy statues do not move!

Romeo: Then don't move, while I kiss you!

[*He kisses her*]

You have taken away my sin[35] with your lips!

Juliet: Then now my lips have the sin they have taken from yours!

Romeo: Sin from my lips? That is terrible! Give me my sin back.

[*He kisses her again*]

Sin from my lips? That is terrible! Give me my sin back.

Juliet: You kiss perfectly – as if you had learned it from a book!
[Nurse comes up to Juliet]

Nurse: Madam, your mother wants to speak to you.

[Juliet moves away towards her mother]

Romeo: *[to Nurse]* Who is her mother?

Nurse: Her mother, young man, is the lady of the house.
She's a good lady. And I am Nurse to her daughter – the
young lady that you were talking to just now. *[Smiles at Romeo
and whispers in his ear]* I tell you, the man who wins her love
will have plenty of money!

Romeo: *[Turning away, shocked]* She is a Capulet! Now my
life is in the hands of my enemy!

Benvolio: *[Coming up to Romeo]* Let's go. The party is over.

Capulet: *[Sees Benvolio and Romeo getting ready to go]* Thank
you for coming and good night, gentlemen. *[to Lady Capulet
and the other guests]* Come on, then, let's all go to bed. It's very
late, I must go and get some sleep.

*[Exit Capulet, Lady Capulet, Romeo and his friends and the other
guests]*

Juliet: Come here, Nurse. *[Watching the guests leaving and
pointing at Romeo]* Who is that gentleman – the man who
wouldn't dance?

Nurse: I don't know.

Juliet: Go and ask his name, Nurse. *[to herself]* If he is
married I think I will die!

Nurse: *[Coming back]* His name is Romeo, and he is a
Montague! He is the only son of your great enemy.

Juliet: The only man I have ever loved is from the only
family I have ever hated! I fell in love with him without
knowing who he is. And now it is too late. Oh, what a way to
fall in love for the first time!

Nurse: *His name is Romeo, and a Montague,*
The only son of your great enemy.
Juliet: *My only love sprung from my only hate.*
Too early seen unknown, and known too late.
Prodigious birth of love it is to me
That I must love a loathed enemy.

sprung from = come from
prodigious = very great
loathed = hated

[Someone calls Juliet from inside the house]
Nurse: *[Calling inside]* We're coming! *[to Juliet]* Come on, let's go. The guests have all gone home.
[Exit Juliet and Nurse]

Act 2, Scene 1

[Near the Capulets' house. Enter Romeo]

Romeo: How can I go home when my heart is here? *[Turns around]* I must go back, and find my love.

[Hears Benvolio and Mercutio coming, and climbs over the garden wall to hide. Enter Benvolio and Mercutio]

Benvolio: *[Calling]* Romeo! My cousin Romeo! Romeo!

Mercutio: He's a sensible man. He's gone home to bed.

Benvolio: No, he ran this way and climbed over the garden wall. Call him with me, good Mercutio.

Mercutio: *[Calling]* Romeo! Lover-boy! I call you in the name of Rosaline's bright eyes, her red lips, her long legs . . .

Benvolio: Stop it, Mercutio! If he hears you, he will be angry. *[Looks around for Romeo and then gives up]* Oh, let's go. He's probably hiding among the trees somewhere. It's no good looking for him when he doesn't want to be found.

[Exit Benvolio and Mercutio]

[Romeo comes forward. He is standing beneath a window of the Capulets' house]

Romeo: Mercutio is making fun of wounds[36] that do not hurt.

[Juliet opens a window above and looks out]

[Seeing Juliet, and whispering] Oh, what is the light coming through that window? The window is the east, and Juliet is the sun! Rise, beautiful sun, and kill the jealous moon! The moon is pale and sick with sadness because you are more beautiful than her. *[Juliet comes forward onto the balcony[37]]* It is my lady! Oh, it is my love! I wish that she knew she was my love! She looks as if she wants to say something. Shall I say something to her? *[Stops himself]* No, she is not talking to me.

She is talking to the stars. Two of the most beautiful stars in the sky have to go away. And they are asking her eyes to shine for them until they come back. What would happen if her eyes could change places with those stars? Next to her bright cheeks, the stars would look dull in her face. They would be like lamps shining next to bright daylight. But if her eyes shone in the sky, they would shine so brightly that all the birds would sing. They would think that it was day, not night. *[Juliet rests her face in her hands]* She rests her cheek in her hand. Oh, I wish that I were a glove on her hand, so that I could touch that cheek.

Juliet: *[Not knowing that Romeo is there]* Oh my!

Romeo: *[Whispering]* She speaks! Oh speak again, bright angel[38]. For watching you from below is like watching an angel sail around on great white clouds.

Juliet: *[to herself]* Oh Romeo, Romeo, why does your name have to be Romeo? Tell me that Montague is not your father, and that that is not your name. Or, if you won't do that, just promise to be my love, and I shall no longer be a Capulet.

Juliet: *O Romeo, Romeo, wherefore art thou Romeo?*
Deny thy father and refuse thy name.
Or if thou wilt not, be but sworn my love
And I'll no longer be a Capulet.

wherefore = why
art = are
thou = you
deny = (in this case) to say you do not know someone
thy = your
refuse = to say no to
wilt = will
but = just
sworn = promised

Romeo: *[to himself]* Should I say something, or should I wait?

Juliet: *[to herself]* It is only your name that is my enemy. If you had another name you would still be the same person. A rose would still smell as sweet, if it were called something different. And Romeo would still be as perfect, even if he were not called Romeo. Give up your name, Romeo – it is not part of you, anyway – and take me instead.

Romeo: *[to Juliet, loudly]* Just call me 'love', and I shall never be Romeo again.

Juliet: *[Shocked that someone is listening to her]* Who is that, hiding in the night and listening to my private talk?

Romeo: I cannot tell you my name. My name, holy statue, is hateful to me because it is an enemy to you. If it were written on paper, I would tear it up.

Juliet: You have only said a few words, but I know your voice already. Aren't you Romeo, and a Montague?

Romeo: I am neither, fair lady, if you dislike either of them.

Juliet: How did you get here, and why did you come? The orchard[39] walls are high and difficult to climb. And if my family find you here, they will kill you.

Romeo: Love's light wings helped me to fly over the walls. Stone walls cannot keep love out. Love is brave enough to try anything – so your family will not stop me.

Juliet: The mask of night is covering my face tonight. If it were not, you would see me blush[40] about the things that you heard me say. I should say that they are not true, I know. But for once, I'm not going to worry about behaving properly. Do you love me? Oh, gentle Romeo, if you do, tell me honestly. If you think I have been won too easily, I'll frown[41] and say no, and you can try to win my love. But otherwise I am not going to pretend. Believe me, other women may be better at

29

hiding their feelings, but I shall be more true than they could ever be. Don't think that I have given in[42] to you so quickly because my love for you is light.

Romeo: Lady, I swear[43] to you by the moon, which lights up the tops of these fruit-trees . . .

Juliet: Oh, don't swear by the moon, which changes all through the month. I don't want your love to be changeable like the moon. If you must swear, swear by yourself. For you are the god that I love. And I'll believe you.

Romeo: If my sweet love . . .

Juliet: *[Interrupting him]* No, do not swear! Although I love you, this is too sudden. It is too much like lightning, which is gone before you notice it. Sweet, good night. This bud of love may have grown into a beautiful flower when we next meet. Good night, good night. Sleep as sweetly as I will.

Romeo: Don't go like this! Let us make a faithful[44] vow of love to each other.

Juliet: I had already given you my vow, even before you asked for it. *[Looks back in through her window]* I hear some noise inside. Dear love, goodbye.

[Nurse calls inside]

[Calling to Nurse] I'm coming, good Nurse! *[to Romeo]* Sweet Montague, be true. Stay there, I'll come back in a moment.

[Exit Juliet]

Romeo: Oh wonderful, wonderful night! I am afraid that this is all a dream. It is too perfect to be true.

[Enter Juliet above]

Juliet: I shall just say one thing, dear Romeo, and then we must say good night. If you are honourable with your love, and want to marry me, I will send a messenger[45] to you tomorrow. Tell the messenger when and where we shall be married. And I shall come to you. I will give you my life, and follow you throughout the world.

Nurse: [*Calling more loudly from inside*] Madam!

Juliet: [*Calling inside to Nurse*] I'm coming! Just a minute! [*to Romeo*] But if you are not honourable, then please . . .

Nurse: [*From inside, impatiently*] Madam!

Juliet: [*to Nurse*] Yes, yes! Just one moment! [*to Romeo*] . . . leave me to my sadness. I shall send the messenger tomorrow. A thousand times good night!

[*Exit Juliet*]

Romeo: The night is a thousand times darker without your light! [*Turning slowly to go*] Lovers are like schoolchildren. When they are about to see each other, they are as excited as children coming home from school. But when they have to say goodbye, they are like children in the morning, on their way to school. Slow and heavy.

[*Enter Juliet again, above*]

Juliet: [*Calling quietly*] Romeo! Romeo!

Romeo: [*Turning back*] My love.

Juliet: What time tomorrow shall I send my messenger to you?

Romeo: By nine o'clock.

Juliet: I will not forget. Oh, it is twenty years until then. [*After a moment*] I have forgotten why I called you back!

Romeo: Let me stand here until you remember.

Juliet: But then I shall keep forgetting, just to make you stand there longer.

Romeo: And I shall keep standing here so that you keep forgetting.

Juliet: It is almost morning. I should make you go. Good night, good night. It is so hard to leave you that I could keep saying good night until the morning.

[Exit Juliet]

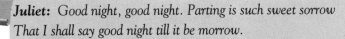

Juliet: *Good night, good night. Parting is such sweet sorrow*
That I shall say good night till it be morrow.

parting = going away from each other
sorrow = sadness
morrow = tomorrow, the next day

Romeo: Let there be sleep in your eyes, and peace in your heart. Morning is smiling on the heavy night, and light is breaking up the eastern clouds. I shall go and see Friar Laurence at the abbey[46]. I will tell him what has happened and ask him for help.

[Exit Romeo]

Act 2, Scene 2

[Near the abbey. Enter Friar Laurence, picking wild flowers]

Friar Laurence: Before the night's dew has dried, I must collect these flowers with their precious juices. Some of them can make people better when they are ill, and some can help people feel stronger. There's nothing on this earth that doesn't do some good. But there's nothing that is so good that it can't be used wrongly.

[Enter Romeo]

[Friar Laurence, not seeing Romeo, bends over and picks a flower]

This flower can make people feel better but it is also a

Before the night's dew has dried, I must collect these flowers with their precious juices.

poison[47]. If you smell it, it makes you feel happy. But if you eat it, you will die. People, like flowers, can be like this. They can be a mixture[48] of good and bad. And when the bad becomes stronger than the good, death slowly eats them.

[Romeo comes forward]

Romeo: Good morning, Father.

Friar Laurence: Good morning. Who is that greeting me so politely? *[Stands up and sees Romeo]* Why are you up so early, my good son? Young people should sleep a golden sleep at night. So I'm sure, if you are up this early, that you must have a troubled mind. *[Romeo shakes his head]* Or if that's not right . . . then I would guess that Romeo didn't go to bed last night!

Romeo: You are right, Father. I enjoyed something much better than sleep.

Friar Laurence: *[Shocked]* God forgive[49] us! Were you with Rosaline?

Romeo: With Rosaline? No, no, Father. I have forgotten that name, and its unhappiness.

Friar Laurence: Oh, good son. But then where have you been?

Romeo: I have been at a party – with my enemy. *[Friar Laurence looks worried]* I have not come to you full of hate, Father. I have fallen in love with the fair daughter of rich Capulet. She has given me her heart, just as I have given her mine. And we are joined together as one in every way except in holy marriage. And now I hope that you will join us in that way too. I shall tell you more about when and where and how we met and fell in love. But first, please promise to marry us today.

Friar Laurence: Holy St Francis! What a change! Is

Rosaline, who you loved so deeply, so quickly forgotten? Young men's love must be in their eyes, not their hearts. All those tears you wasted on Rosaline! The sun still hasn't cleared your sighs from the sky. I can still hear your cries of sadness in my old ears. *[Touches Romeo's face]* And there on your cheek is the stain[50] of a tear that hasn't washed off yet. All that sadness was for Rosaline. And now you've changed, have you?

Friar Laurence: *Holy Saint Francis! What a change is here!*
Is Rosaline, that thou didst love so dear,
So soon forsaken? Young men's love then lies
Not truly in their hearts but in their eyes.
Jesu Maria! What a deal of brine
Hath wash'd thy sallow cheeks for Rosaline.

thou = you
didst = did
forsaken = given up, forgotten
Jesu Maria = an exclamation, like Goodness me!
What a deal of = What a lot of
brine = salt water (here, tears)
hath = has
wash'd = washed
thy = your
sallow = pale yellow, unhealthy

Romeo: You often told me off[51] for loving Rosaline.

Friar Laurence: For doting on[52] her, not for loving her.

Romeo: And you told me to forget about my love.

Friar Laurence: Yes, but not to forget about one love and find another straight away.

Romeo: Don't tell me off, Father. This is different. I love her and she loves me. Rosaline never loved me.

Friar Laurence: No, because she knew that you didn't even understand what love is. *[Making a decision]* Well, come with me, young man. I shall do this for you for one reason: perhaps this marriage will turn your families' hatred for each other into love.

Romeo: *[Excited]* Oh, let's go! As quickly as possible!

Friar Laurence: *[Calmly]* Slowly and sensibly. People who run too fast fall over.

Act 2, Scene 3

[Near Romeo's house. Enter Benvolio and Mercutio]

Mercutio: Where can Romeo be? Did he not go home last night?

Benvolio: Not to his father's house, no. I asked his servant. Tybalt, Capulet's nephew, has sent a letter to Romeo's house.

Mercutio: It must be a challenge[53]! He is challenging Romeo to fight with him!

Benvolio: Romeo will take the challenge.

Mercutio: But poor Romeo is already dead. He has been stabbed by the dark eyes of that woman. His heart has been torn apart by love. And anyway, could he really fight Tybalt?

Benvolio: Why, what is so special about Tybalt?

Mercutio: Oh, Tybalt knows everything about fighting. Every move he makes is perfectly timed. *[Mercutio pretends to fight with a sword]* He waits for a moment: one, two . . . *[Mercutio stands still, holding his 'sword' up]* then, three! – he stabs you in the heart! *[He stabs his 'sword' at Benvolio]*

[Enter Romeo]

Benvolio: Here comes Romeo! Here comes Romeo!

Mercutio: *[Laughing]* I expect he has come to tell us poems about his love. Romeo! Where were you last night?

Romeo: I'm sorry. I had something important to do.

[Enter Nurse, holding a fan]

Mercutio: Ah, who's this? I'm glad she has a fan to hide behind. Because her fan is prettier than her face!

Nurse: Good morning, gentlemen.

Mercutio: Good afternoon, madam.

Nurse: Is it afternoon already?

Mercutio: Oh yes. It is exactly twelve o'clock. Those clock hands are pointing right up. *[He sticks two fingers up in a rude way]*

Nurse: *[Shocked]* Well, really. What sort of man are you?

Romeo: *[Laughing]* One who has made himself bad, madam.

Nurse: Yes, I can see that. Now, can you tell me where I can find young Romeo?

Romeo: I am Romeo.

Nurse: Sir, I would like to have a quiet talk with you.

Mercutio: *[Laughing rudely]* Oh, Romeo, a quiet talk! *[Turns to go with Benvolio]* Are you coming back to your father's house? We're going there for lunch.

Romeo: I'll see you there later.

Mercutio: *[In a joking way]* Goodbye, lady, lady, lady.

[Exit Mercutio and Benvolio]

Nurse: Well, really! Who is that rude man, sir?

Romeo: A gentleman who likes the sound of his own voice too much, Nurse.

Nurse: *[Fanning herself crossly]* Rude young man. I am so cross that I am shaking all over. *[Turns to Romeo]* Now, sir, my young lady asked me to come and find you. But first let me tell you this. If you treat her badly, it would be a terrible thing to do. She is very young, you know.

Romeo: Nurse, please give my greetings to your lady. And let me say honestly . . .

Nurse: *[Claps her hands with excitement]* Oh, I'll tell her! Goodness me, she will be a happy woman!

Romeo: What will you tell her, Nurse? I haven't finished saying it yet.

Nurse: I will tell her, sir, that you say 'honestly'. And that, to me, means that you are asking her to marry you.

Romeo: *[Smiling]* Tell her to come to the abbey this afternoon. *[Excited]* And there, Friar Laurence will marry us! *[Gives Nurse some money]* Thank you for your help.

Nurse: Oh, no, sir, I couldn't.

Romeo: Yes, yes, you must.

[Nurse puts the money in her pocket, looking pleased]

Nurse: This afternoon, you said, sir? Well, she shall be there.

Romeo: Go now, good Nurse, and wait behind the abbey wall. My servant will come and meet you there, and he will bring you a rope ladder[54]. I shall use the ladder to climb up to your lady's room tonight. Goodbye. Give my greetings to your lady for me.

Nurse: Oh yes, a thousand greetings!

[Exit Nurse]

Act 2, Scene 4

[Juliet's room in the Capulets' house. Enter Juliet]

Juliet: *[Walking impatiently backwards and forwards]* It was nine o'clock when I sent Nurse to see Romeo. She promised that she would be back in half an hour. *[Suddenly worried]* Perhaps she wasn't able to meet him. No, of course she was. Oh, she is too slow. Love's messengers should be ten times faster than the sun which pushes the darkness back across the hills. The sun is high in the sky, and it is three hours since nine o'clock, but still she has not come back.

[Enter Nurse]

Oh, here she comes! *[Juliet rushes over to Nurse, and takes her hands]* Oh sweet Nurse, what news do you have? Did you see him? *[Nurse pretends to look sad]* Oh, why do you look so sad? If you have bad news, you should tell it with a smile. And if it is good news, you are spoiling it with your unhappy face.

Nurse: *[Sighing and sitting down heavily]* I'm so tired. Leave me alone for a moment. *[Taking off her shoes and rubbing*[55] *her feet]* Oh, my feet hurt.

Juliet: I wish you had my feet, and I had your news. Come on, Nurse – good, good Nurse, please speak.

Nurse: Goodness me, what a rush. Can't you wait for a moment? Don't you see that I am out of breath?

Juliet: *[Impatiently]* How can you be out of breath? You have enough breath to tell me that you are out of breath! You've taken such a long time explaining why you can't give me the news. It would be much quicker just to give me the news itself! *[Calming down a little]* Is the news good or bad? Just say which, and then I'll wait to hear all about it. Please just tell me that. Is it good or bad?

Nurse: Well, you have made a silly choice. You don't know how to choose a man! Romeo? No, not him! *[Smiling]* I agree his face is better than any man's, and his legs. And his body – you certainly can't compare it with anyone else's. He is not the flower of politeness, but I agree he's gentle as a lamb. *[Enjoying keeping Juliet waiting]* Well, off you go, girl. Did you have dinner at home?

Juliet: What? No, no, I didn't. But I knew all these things before. What does Romeo say about our marriage? What about that?

Nurse: *[Rubbing her head]* Oh, I have got a headache. I feel as if my head is about to break into twenty pieces. And my back – oh, my back. You should feel terrible for sending me off like that, and making me walk all over the place.

Juliet: I am really sorry that you aren't feeling well. *[Kneels[56] on the floor in front of Nurse's chair]* But sweet, sweet, sweet Nurse, tell me, what does my love say?

Nurse: *[Stops rubbing her head and back, and smiles]* Will your mother let you go to the abbey today?

Juliet: Yes.

Nurse: Then when you get there, go to Friar Laurence's room. A husband will be waiting there to make you into a wife. *[Juliet jumps up, excited]* Now I can see some blood in your cheeks! Off you go. I'm going to fetch a ladder. Your love is going to use it to climb up to your room when it is dark. Goodness me, I'm like your servant, working to keep you happy. Now I'm going to go and have some dinner. Off you go to find Friar Laurence.

Juliet: Oh, happy news! Honest Nurse, goodbye.

[Exit Juliet and Nurse]

Act 2, Scene 5

[At the abbey. Enter Friar Laurence and Romeo]

Friar Laurence: I hope that God will smile upon this holy marriage, and that we will not be punished with sorrow[57] for it later.

Romeo: To be with Juliet just for one minute fills me with joy[58]. And no sorrow could ever be greater than that joy. Marry us with your holy words, I ask you, Father. Then death, which eats away at love, can do what it wants. It is enough for me that I can call her mine.

Friar Laurence: Love that is so strong often comes to a terrible end. It dies out when it reaches its highest point, just like fire. So try to love gently. Gentle love lasts longer. And remember that you don't get somewhere more quickly by going too fast.

[Enter Juliet. Romeo takes her in his arms]

Juliet: Good afternoon, Father.

Friar Laurence: Romeo will greet you for me, daughter.

[Romeo gives Juliet a long kiss]

Juliet: I think Romeo has greeted me for himself, too! And so I should return his greeting.

[She kisses him]

Romeo: Oh Juliet, is your heart full of joy like mine? You can describe the rich colours of our happiness better than I can. Sweeten the air with your breath, and tell the world how happy this meeting makes us both.

Juliet: Words cannot say how rich our happiness is. And I do feel like a rich person. I cannot tell you how much love I have, because I have so much.

Friar Laurence: Come with me and let us marry you quickly. For you two must not be alone together until the holy church has made you one.

Act 3, Scene 1

[*The streets of Verona. Enter Mercutio, Benvolio and their servants*]

Benvolio: Come on, good Mercutio, let's go home. It is such a hot day, and the Capulets are in town. If we meet them, we shall not get away without a fight. For this hot weather stirs up the mad blood in everybody.

Mercutio: Well, look who's talking!

Benvolio: [*Surprised*] What do you mean?

Mercutio: Come, come! Your temper is as hot as anyone's. You will argue with someone because he has more hair in his beard than you. You will argue with a man for coughing in the street, because his cough has woken your dog! And here you are telling me not to get into a fight.

Benvolio: [*Laughing*] If I argued as much as you do, my life would not be worth very much – for it would not last very long!

[*Enter Tybalt and his servants*]

Benvolio: Oh no, here come the Capulets.

[*Tries to pull Mercutio away*]

Mercutio: I don't care! I'm not going anywhere!

Tybalt: Good afternoon, gentlemen. May I speak with one of you for a moment?

Mercutio: Are you sure you only want to speak? How about fighting, too?

Tybalt: If you give me a reason for that, you will find that I am quite ready, sir.

[*Enter Romeo*]

Ah, here's the man I want to talk to. Romeo, you are a villain.

43

Romeo: Tybalt, it is only because I have a reason to love you that I can control my anger at that greeting. I am not a villain. So goodbye. You do not know me. *[Turns to go]*

Tybalt: Nothing can right the wrong you have done me. Turn and take out your sword!

Romeo: I tell you that I have never wronged you. I have more reasons to love you than you could know. So, forget all this, good Capulet – your name is as important to me as my own.

Mercutio: *[Angrily]* Oh how calmly and dishonourably you give in to him! *[He takes out his sword]* Tybalt, you rat-catcher, will you fight?

Tybalt: What do you want from me?

Mercutio: Your life! Now will you take out your sword? Be quick, or I shall cut off your ears first.

Tybalt: I shall fight you. *[He takes out his sword]*

Romeo: Gentle Mercutio, put your sword away.

Mercutio: *[to Tybalt]* Come on, sir, let's see these clever moves everyone talks about so much.

[They fight]

Romeo: *[Holding up his sword]* Take out your sword, Benvolio. Let's knock down their swords. Gentlemen, stop this! *[Romeo tries to stop them fighting with his sword]* Tybalt, Mercutio! The Prince has told you never to fight like this in the streets of Verona. Stop, Tybalt! Good Mercutio!

[Romeo stands between them, and Tybalt steps forward and stabs Mercutio under Romeo's arm. Mercutio falls to the ground. Exit Tybalt]

Mercutio: I am hurt. Damn[59] both your families! I am dying. *[Looks for Tybalt]* Has he gone? Did I not hurt him at all? *[Holds his wound]*

Romeo: [*Hurrying to Mercutio's side*] Be brave, man. The wound cannot be too bad.

Mercutio: Oh, it is enough, it will do. Ask for me tomorrow and you will find me a grave[60] man. Damn both your families! [*to Romeo*] Why did you stand between us? I was hurt under your arm.

Romeo: I thought it was the best thing to do.

Mercutio: [*Crying out with pain*] Get me into someone's house, Benvolio. Damn both your families! They have made me into worm's meat.

[*Exit Benvolio, holding Mercutio*]

Romeo: [*Falling onto his knees, upset*] This gentleman is one of the Prince's own family, and my great friend. He has been terribly wounded, and all for me. All because Tybalt spoke against me – Tybalt who just an hour ago became my cousin. Oh sweet Juliet, your beauty has made me weak. It has softened my brave spirit[61].

Romeo: *This gentleman, the Prince's near ally,*
My very friend, hath got this mortal hurt
In my behalf – my reputation stain'd
With Tybalt's slander – Tybalt that an hour
Hath been my cousin. O sweet Juliet,
Thy beauty hath made me effeminate
And in my temper soften'd valour's steel.

ally = relative
hath = has
mortal = serious
in my behalf = for me
reputation = what other people think about someone
stain'd = stained, made dirty
slander = saying something about someone that is not true
thy = your
effeminate = like a woman
temper = the way someone behaves
soften'd = softened, made something soft
valour = courage, bravery
steel = a strong metal

[Enter Benvolio]

Benvolio: *[Upset]* Oh Romeo, brave Mercutio is dead.

Romeo: This is a black day, and there will be more black days to come. This is just the beginning of the unhappiness that other days will bring to an end.

[Enter Tybalt]

Benvolio: Here comes the furious Tybalt, back again.

Romeo: Well, now I throw off my gentleness! I am full of fiery anger now! *[to Tybalt]* Tybalt, you called me a villain earlier. Take that back! Either you, or I, or both of us will die with Mercutio.

[They fight. Tybalt falls to the ground, wounded. Romeo stands shocked, not knowing what to do]

Benvolio: Go, Romeo, run away! Tybalt is dead! The Prince will have you killed if he finds you. Go! Go!

[Exit Romeo]

[Enter Prince, Montague, Capulet and their wives]

Prince: *[Angrily]* Who started this hateful fight?

Benvolio: I can tell you everything, my lord. *[Points to Tybalt's body]* This man, who was killed by young Romeo, killed brave Mercutio.

Lady Capulet: *[Falling crying upon Tybalt's body]* Tybalt, my nephew, my brother's child! *[to the Prince]* Oh, Prince, a member of my family has died. And a Montague must die for this. Romeo killed Tybalt. Romeo must not live.

Prince: Romeo killed Tybalt, Tybalt killed Mercutio. So who pays now for dear Mercutio's blood?

Montague: Not Romeo, Prince. He was Mercutio's friend. Tybalt should have been punished, and Romeo has punished him for us.

Prince: And for what he did, I exile[62] him from Verona at once. *[Lady Montague cries out, shocked]* I too have an interest in this bloody fight between you. A member of my family died here today. And so I shall give you a hard punishment that will make you all sorry for my loss. Don't ask me to change my mind. I shall not listen to tears or prayers[63]. Romeo must go from this town. If he is found here, he will die. *[to his servants, pointing at Tybalt's body]* Take this body away. *[Turning to the Montagues and the Capulets]* I cannot forgive people who kill. That would just cause more murder[64].

Act 3, Scene 2

[Juliet's room. Enter Juliet]

Juliet: *[Looking out of her window impatiently]* Come on, night! Come on, Romeo! You will turn my night into day. For you will come shining on the wings of the night like snow on a raven's[65] back. Come on, night, give me my Romeo. And when I die, take him and cut him out into little stars. He will make the sky so beautiful that all the world will be in love with the night. And no one will care about the sun anymore, because it will seem too bright and ugly.

Juliet: *Come night, come Romeo, come thou day in night,*
For thou wilt lie upon the wings of night
Whiter than new snow upon a raven's back.
Come gentle night, come loving black-brow'd night,
Give me my Romeo; and when I shall die
Take him and cut him out in little stars,
And he will make the face of heaven so fine

That all the world will be in love with night,
And pay no worship to the garish sun.

thou = you
wilt = will
black-brow'd = black-browed; with a black forehead
heaven = the sky
pay worship to = to show love and respect for
garish = very bright and colourful in an ugly way

[Enter Nurse, holding a rope ladder, and shaking her head sadly]
Oh, here comes my Nurse. *[Runs to Nurse, excited]* Any news, Nurse? What have you got there? The rope ladder that Romeo told you to bring?

Nurse: *[Still shaking her head]* Yes, yes, the rope ladder.

Juliet: *[Seeing that something is wrong]* What's the matter?

Nurse: *[Crying]* Oh, he's dead, he's dead. Oh terrible day! He's gone, he's killed, he's dead.

Juliet: *[Shocked]* What? Can heaven[66] be so jealous? Has Romeo killed himself? Just say 'yes' and that word will be more full of poison than the most dangerous snake on earth. If he has been killed, say 'yes', and if not, say 'no'.

Nurse: I saw the wound, I saw it with my eyes – here in his heart. *[Puts her hand on her heart]* He was so pale, and covered in blood.

Juliet: *[Crying out]* Oh, break, heart! You have nothing left in this world – break! Hateful body, go back to the earth! Romeo and I will share the same heavy death bed. *[Falls on the floor crying]*

Nurse: *[Still crying, and not listening to Juliet]* Oh Tybalt, Tybalt, the best friend I had. Oh, honourable gentleman! I can't believe that I have lived to see you dead.

Juliet: *[Sitting up, confused]* What storm is this, blowing one way and then the other? Romeo has been killed, and Tybalt is dead? My dearest cousin and my dearer husband? There is no one to live for if those two are gone!

Nurse: *[Finally looking up at Juliet]* Tybalt is dead, and Romeo has been exiled. Romeo, who killed Tybalt, has been exiled.

Juliet: Oh God! Romeo killed Tybalt?

Nurse: *[Starting to cry again]* He did! Oh terrible day!

Juliet: Oh, then, he has the heart of a snake, hidden away by a flowering face! He is a raven with the feathers of a dove! An honourable villain! How can a cruel spirit have such a sweet body? Why was a book so full of hateful things given such a beautiful cover?

Nurse: You can't believe anything about men. They are all bad, they are all liars. *[Sits in her chair]* Where's the servant? *[Calling to servant]* Bring me a strong drink! Oh, all this sorrow is making me old. Shame on Romeo.

Juliet: *[Suddenly standing up, angrily]* What a terrible thing to say! Shame can never sit in his heart – there is only room there for honour. Oh, how wrong I was to be angry with him!

Nurse: How can you say nice things about the man who killed your cousin?

Juliet: How can I say bad things about my own husband? Why did he kill my cousin, like a villain? Because that villain cousin was trying to kill my husband! Away, tears of sorrow! These should be tears of joy! Tybalt tried to kill my husband, but my husband is alive, and Tybalt is dead! All this should make me feel better. So why am I crying? There was something else that you said. It was worse than Tybalt's death, and it is murdering me. I would try to forget it, but like a sinner who has done bad things, I cannot. Tybalt is dead and Romeo – exiled. That is worse than Tybalt being killed ten thousand times. Tybalt's death is bad enough. But Romeo is exiled. There is no end to that word's death. No words can describe the sorrow that word brings. Look at that rope ladder! It was made to bring Romeo to my bed. But it is death, not Romeo, that will come to me in my wedding bed!

Nurse: *[Suddenly feeling sorry for Juliet]* Go to your room. I'll go and find Romeo, and ask him to come and see you. I know where he is. He's hiding in Friar Laurence's room. Your Romeo will be here tonight.

Juliet: *[Gives her a ring]* Oh find him, give him this ring, and tell him to come and say his last goodbye.

[Exit Juliet and Nurse]

Act 3, Scene 3

[At Friar Laurence's room. Enter Friar Laurence]

Friar Laurence: Romeo, come out! *[Enter Romeo, who has been hiding in Friar Laurence's room]* Oh, you poor frightened man. Trouble loves you, doesn't it! Everything you do ends in calamity[67].

Romeo: Father, what's the news? What is the Prince's punishment? What new sorrow is waiting for me?

Friar Laurence: Oh, dear son, you know sorrow too well. But here is the Prince's punishment. He has been gentle with you. He has not punished you with death, but with exile.

Romeo: *[Crying out]* Exile! Have mercy[68], say 'death' instead! For exile is far more terrible than death. Don't say 'exile'.

Friar Laurence: You should be thankful! The proper punishment for what you have done is death. But the kind

Prince has shown mercy on you. Why can't you see that?

Romeo: This is not mercy! Heaven is here, where Juliet lives. The cats, the dogs, the little mice can stay here in heaven and see Juliet. But Romeo may not. Even the flies are more important than Romeo. They can touch her dear white hands. They can steal a kiss from her lips – her lips, which are so perfect that they think touching each other is a sin. But Romeo may not. He is exiled. And yet you still think that exile is not death? Could you not find a way to kill me more quickly? Use poison, or a knife! But don't kill me by telling me that I am 'exiled'! Oh Friar, you are my friend, you are the person I tell my secrets to. How do you have the heart to crush me with that word 'exiled'?

Friar Laurence: *[Trying to be patient]* You are being foolish[69]. Now listen to me.

Romeo: You don't know how I feel! If you were young like me, and in love with Juliet . . . If you had only been married for an hour when Tybalt was murdered . . . If you doted like me, and were exiled like me . . . Well, then you might know! Then you might tear at your hair and fall on the ground like me! *[Romeo falls to the ground, his head in his hands]*

[There is a knock at the door]

Friar Laurence: *[Whispering]* Get up. Someone is knocking at the door. *[Loudly, to the person knocking]* Who's there? *[Whispering angrily to Romeo, who is still lying on the floor]* Romeo, get up, or they will take you away!

[Another knock at the door]

Who is it? What do you want?

Nurse: *[Calling from outside]* Let me in and I shall tell you. I have come from Lady Juliet.

Friar Laurence: Then you are welcome.

[Friar Laurence opens the door. Enter Nurse]

Nurse: Oh holy Friar, tell me. Where is my lady's lord? Where is Romeo?

Friar Laurence: There on the ground, made ill by his own tears.

Nurse: Oh, just like my lady. Just like her. Oh terrible sorrow! Juliet is just like him, lying on the floor crying and crying. *[to Romeo]* Stand up, stand up. Stand and be a man. For Juliet.

[Romeo gets up]

Romeo: Nurse. Were you talking about Juliet? How is she? Does she think that I am a terrible murderer? I have stained the childhood of our joy with blood from her family. Where is she? What does she say about our love, which has been stopped so suddenly like this?

Nurse: Oh, she doesn't say anything, sir. She just cries and cries. One minute she throws herself on her bed, the next she sits up and cries 'Tybalt!' and then 'Romeo!' And then she falls down again.

Romeo: As if that name is murdering her, just as that name's hand murdered her cousin. Oh, tell me, Friar, where in my body can I find my name? Tell me so that I may cut it out!

[He holds up his sword as if he is about to kill himself]

Friar Laurence: Stop, Romeo! I thought you were more sensible than this. You have already killed Tybalt. Are you going to kill yourself too? And kill the lady who lives for you with a terrible act of hate against yourself? Pull yourself together! Your Juliet, for whom you wanted to die a minute ago, is alive. You should be happy about that. Tybalt wanted to kill you, but you killed Tybalt. You should be happy about that, too. You could have been punished with death, but you have just been exiled. And you should be happy about that as well.

[Romeo sits up, listening to Friar Laurence] Many good things have happened to you. But like a badly-behaved child, you get angry at what happens to you and your love. Be careful, because people who behave in that way die in sadness. Go and find Juliet as we had planned. Go and make her feel better. But make sure you leave before dawn, or you will not be able to get to Mantua. That is where you must live, for now. Then one day, hopefully, you can ask the Prince for forgiveness. Then you will be able to tell everyone about your marriage. You will come back with twenty hundred thousand times more joy than the sorrow you are leaving with. Go ahead of him, Nurse. Give my greetings to your lady. And tell her to try and make everyone in the house, so full of sadness, go to bed early. Romeo is coming.

Nurse: Oh, what good advice! My lord, I'll tell my lady you will come.

Romeo: *[Standing up, helped by Friar Laurence's words]* Yes, do. And tell my sweet to prepare to be angry with me.

[Nurse starts to leave, but remembers something and turns back]

Nurse: *[Giving Romeo the ring from Juliet]* Oh sir, here's a ring she asked me to give you. Be quick, for it is getting very late.

Romeo: Oh, this takes away so much of my sadness.

Friar Laurence: Off you go. When you get to Mantua, I shall send news to your servant. Give me your hand. It is late. Good night, and goodbye.

Romeo: *[Taking Friar Laurence's hand]* I am sorry to leave you, Friar – but the greatest joy of all is waiting for me. Goodbye.

[Exit Nurse, Romeo and Friar Laurence]

Act 3, Scene 4

[Juliet's room. Enter Romeo and Juliet, standing at the window]

Juliet: Do you have to go already? It is a long time till day. That was a nightingale[70] we heard singing, not a lark[71]. She sits on that tree and sings every night. Believe me, love, it was a nightingale.

> **Juliet:** *Wilt thou be gone? It is not yet near day.*
> *It was the nightingale and not the lark*
> *That pierc'd the fearful hollow of thine ear.*
> *Nightly she sings on yond pomegranate tree.*
> *Believe me, love, it was the nightingale.*
>
> *wilt* = will
> *thou* = you
> *pierc'd* = pierced, made a hole in
> hollow = hole
> *thine* = your
> *yond* = that
> pomegranate = a large round fruit with hard skin

Romeo: It was no nightingale. It was the lark, who starts singing when morning is coming. *[Points through the window]* Look, love, the light is breaking up the clouds over there in the east. Night's candles have burned out, and day is looking out over the mountain tops. I must go and live, or stay and die.

Juliet: That light is not daylight. It is a special light that the sun breathes out to guide you to Mantua. So stay. You don't need to go yet.

Romeo: Let them take me, and kill me. I am happy with that, if you are. I'll say that that light is not the eye of the morning, and I'll say that that sound is not the song of the lark. I want to stay; I cannot make myself go. Come, death, and welcome. That is what Juliet wants, too. Let's talk, my love. It is not day.

Juliet: [*Suddenly worried*] It is, it is. Go! It is the lark, singing such an ugly song. Go, go. It is getting lighter and lighter.

Romeo: Lighter and lighter. As our sorrows get darker and darker.

[*Enter Nurse, in a hurry*]

Nurse: Madam.

Juliet: Nurse?

Nurse: Your mother is coming to your room. It is nearly day, be careful.

[*Exit Nurse*]

Juliet: Then, window, let day in and let my life out.

Romeo: Goodbye, goodbye. One kiss and I'll be gone.

[They kiss, and Romeo climbs down the rope ladder]

Juliet: Have you really gone, just like that? My love, my lord, my husband, my friend – I must hear from you every hour of every day. For there are many days in one minute without you. And that means I shall be old before I see my Romeo again.

Romeo: Goodbye. I shall send news to you whenever I can.

Juliet: Oh, do you think we will ever meet again?

Romeo: I know that we will. And all these sorrows will just be things that we talk about.

Juliet: Oh God, I have a terrible feeling. Now that you are down there, you look like a dead person at the bottom of a tomb. You look so pale.

Romeo: And believe me, love, so do you. Sorrow is drinking our blood. Goodbye! Goodbye!

[Exit Romeo]

Juliet: *[Crying]* Oh, people say that fortune[72] is always changing its mind. Well, then, change your mind now, fortune. And send him back to me.

[Enter Lady Capulet]

Lady Capulet: Are you awake, Juliet?

Juliet: It is my mother. What can she want?

[Juliet goes down from the window]

Lady Capulet: How are you, Juliet?

[Enter Juliet, crying]

Juliet: I am not well, Madam.

Lady Capulet: Still crying for your cousin's death? Are you trying to wash him out of his grave with tears? A little sadness is good, because it shows that you loved someone. But too much sorrow seems like foolishness.

Juliet: I cannot stop crying for what I have lost.

Lady Capulet: Well, I have come to bring you some happy news, my girl.

Juliet: We need some happy news at a time like this. What is it, Mother?

Lady Capulet: To help you forget your sorrow, your kind father has arranged a surprise day of great happiness.

Juliet: That is good news! What day is that?

Lady Capulet: *[Excited]* Early next Thursday morning, that honourable young gentleman, Count Paris, will marry you at St Peter's Church!

Juliet: *[Shocked]* By St Peter's Church, he will not! *[Calming herself down a little]* Why is this all so quick? How can I marry someone who hasn't tried to win my love yet? Please tell my lord and father, madam, that I will not marry yet. And when I do marry, I swear that I would rather marry Romeo than Paris. And you know how much I hate Romeo!

Lady Capulet: *[Sighing]* Here comes your father. Tell him that yourself, and see what he says.

[Enter Capulet and Nurse]

Capulet: How are you, Juliet? Still crying? Your little body is like a small boat, and your eyes are like the sea. And if there isn't a sudden calm, your tears and the winds of your sighs will knock you over. *[to his wife]* Well, my dear. Have you told her about our decision?

Lady Capulet: *[Sighing]* Yes, sir, but she says she will not marry Paris. The silly girl should just get married to her grave!

Capulet: *[Not believing what he has heard]* What? Wait a minute. Let me try and understand this. Is she not full of thanks? Is she not pleased? Does she not feel glad that we have found such an honourable husband for her?

Juliet: No, I am not pleased, because I hate the idea of this marriage. But I am thankful, because I know that you were only trying to make me happy.

Capulet: *[Very angry]* What's all this? Not pleased but thankful? Well, forget about your 'not pleased's and your 'thankful's! Get yourself ready to marry Paris at St Peter's Church on Thursday, or I shall take you there myself! You pale-faced fool!

Lady Capulet: *[to Capulet]* You are too full of anger.

Capulet: Oh, it makes me mad! I have worked so hard to find her a good husband. And now that I've found a young gentleman from a good family, that silly fool says, 'I won't marry him, I can't love him, I'm too young.' *[Turning to Juliet]* Well, believe me, if you won't marry him, this is not your home any more. I don't care if you die in the streets! For you shall never have anything of mine again.

[Exit Capulet]

Juliet: *[Putting her head on the floor and crying]* Is there no pity[73] sitting in the clouds that sees to the bottom of my sorrow? *[Sits up and takes her mother's hand]* Oh, sweet mother, please stop this marriage, just for a month, or a week. Or if you can't, you must make the wedding bed in the tomb where Tybalt lies!

Lady Capulet: *[Pushing Juliet away and getting up]* Don't talk to me! I have nothing to say to you. Do what you want. I've had enough of you!

[Exit Lady Capulet]

Juliet: Oh God, oh Nurse, what can I do? I already have a husband, I have taken my marriage vows. Make me feel better. Tell me what to do!

Nurse: *[Thinking for a moment]* Romeo is exiled. I'm sure that he won't come back and make trouble for you. So I think it's best that you marry the Count. *[Juliet looks up, shocked]* Oh, he's a lovely gentleman. Romeo's nothing compared to him. This is a very good marriage – better than your first, actually. And even if it isn't, your first husband is dead, or it is like he is dead. He's certainly no use to you here.

Juliet: *[Shocked, but pretending[74] to listen to Nurse]* Is that what you really think?

Nurse: I mean it from the bottom of my heart.

Juliet: *[Pretending]* Well, I feel much better now, thank you. Please tell my mother that I am going to see Friar Laurence. I want to ask for forgiveness for upsetting my father.

Nurse: *[Pleased]* Of course I will. Oh, you've done the right thing!

[Exit Nurse]

Juliet: That bad old woman! How can she want me to marry Paris? And how can she talk about Romeo like that, after she's said so many good things about him before? Off you go, Nurse! I shall never share my secrets with you again. Now I'll go and see Friar Laurence, and ask him what I should do. And if he can't help me, I am not afraid to die.

Act 4, Scene 1

[At Friar Laurence's. Enter Friar Laurence and Paris]

Friar Laurence: *[Worried]* You say that you want to get married on Thursday, sir? That's very soon.

Paris: That is what my Lord Capulet wants. And I certainly don't want to slow him down.

Friar Laurence: *[to himself]* But I know why he must be slowed down. *[Sees Juliet coming, and turns to Paris]* Look, sir, here comes the lady.

[Enter Juliet]

Paris: I'm so happy to see you, my lady and my wife.

Juliet: You may be happy to see me when I am a wife.

Paris: You will be a wife, my love, on Thursday.

Juliet: Whatever must happen will happen. *[to Friar Laurence]* Do you have a moment to talk, holy Father, or shall I come and see you this evening?

Friar Laurence: I am free now, daughter. *[to Paris]* My lord, I must ask you to leave us alone.

Paris: Of course. Juliet, I shall wake you early on Thursday. Until then, goodbye, and keep this holy kiss. *[He kisses her hand]*

[Exit Paris]

Juliet: *[Starting to cry]* Oh, shut the door, and when you have done that, come and cry with me. There is no hope for me, no help!

Friar Laurence: Oh Juliet, I already know why you are so full of sorrow. It hurts me to think about it, too. I hear you must be married to this Count next Thursday.

Juliet: Oh Friar, tell me how I can stop this marriage. Or if you can't help me, let me use this knife to end it all. *[Takes* *out a knife]* God joined my heart and Romeo's. You joined our hands in marriage. And I would rather kill my hand and my heart than give them to another man.

Friar Laurence: Wait, daughter. I have thought of something. It is a desperate[75] thing to do. You say that you would rather kill yourself than marry Count Paris. In that case, you are probably strong enough to try something that is a little like death. If you are brave enough to do it, I shall tell you how.

Juliet: Oh, tell me to jump off the highest wall, or to sit in a bed of snakes. Tie me up with roaring bears, or tell me to lie with a dead man in his new-made grave. Before, I was frightened just to hear about such things. But now I would do them without any fear[76], so that I can be a faithful wife to my sweet love.

Friar Laurence: Well, then, go home and tell your father that you will marry Paris. It is Wednesday tomorrow. Make sure that you are alone in your room tomorrow night – don't let your Nurse stay with you. Take this bottle with you. *[He takes out a bottle of liquid]* And when you are in bed, drink the mixture[77]. It will run through your body and make you cold and sleepy. It will seem as if you have stopped breathing. Your lips and cheeks will go pale and your body will go cold and hard. When Paris comes to wake you up on the morning of your marriage, he will think you are dead. And then you will be carried to the Capulets' tomb, dressed in your best clothes, like a dead person. But when everyone has left, you will wake up, feeling as if you have had a lovely sleep. And Romeo and I will be waiting there for you. I shall write to him now and tell him what we are doing. That same night, he will take you away to Mantua. If you are not too frightened to do this, it will free you from this marriage to Paris.

Juliet: *[Putting her hand out for the bottle, excited]* Give it to me! Give it to me! Don't talk to me about being frightened!

Friar Laurence: Here you are. *[He gives her the bottle]* Off you go! Be brave, and I hope that this plan will be successful. I shall send a friar to Mantua with a letter for your husband.

Juliet: Love will give me strength. Goodbye, dear Father.

[Exit Juliet and Friar Laurence]

Act 4, Scene 2

[Enter Capulet, Lady Capulet, Nurse and Servants]

Capulet: *[to Nurse]* So, has my daughter gone to see Friar Laurence?

Nurse: Yes, she has.

Capulet: Well, perhaps he will do her some good. What an annoying useless girl she is! Always trying to get what she wants!

[Enter Juliet]

Nurse: Here she comes now, looking very happy.

Capulet: There you are, my girl. Where have you been?

Juliet: I have been learning that I should always do what you tell me. Friar Laurence has told me to come and ask you to forgive me. I am sorry, father. I will always obey you from now on. *[She kneels on the floor]*

Capulet: *[Takes her hand and smiles] [Calling out]* Go and tell the Count this news! We won't wait until Thursday. I'll have these two married tomorrow morning.

Juliet: I met the young lord at Friar Laurence's. And I spoke to him with love.

Capulet: *[Pleased]* Well, I am glad! This is good. Stand up. *[Juliet gets up] [Turning to Lady Capulet and Nurse]* We have a lot to thank this holy friar for.

Juliet: Nurse, will you go and help me find something to wear tomorrow?

Lady Capulet: *[to Capulet]* Why don't we wait till Thursday? That's soon enough.

Capulet: No, we'll go to church tomorrow. Go, Nurse, go with her.

[Exit Juliet and Nurse]

Lady Capulet: We shall never be ready in time. It is nearly night already.

Capulet: Don't worry, I shall hurry around getting things ready, and it will all be fine, I promise you. Now go to Juliet, and help to get her ready. I won't go to bed tonight, leave it all to me. Anyone there? *[Calling to the servants]* They've all gone out. Well, I shall go and see Count Paris myself, and tell him about tomorrow. Oh, my heart is wonderfully light now that my girl has come back to us.

[Exit Capulet and Lady Capulet]

Act 4, Scene 3

[Juliet's room. Enter Juliet and Nurse, holding up clothes and looking at them]

Juliet: Yes, these things are fine. But gentle Nurse, please leave me on my own tonight. I have many prayers to say so that heaven will smile on me. For I am full of sin at the moment, as you know.

[Enter Lady Capulet]

64

Lady Capulet: Are you busy? Do you need any help?

Juliet: No madam, we've found everything we need. So please leave me alone now. Let Nurse stay up with you tonight. I am sure you will need her help to get everything done.

Lady Capulet: *[Kissing Juliet]* Good night. Go to bed and rest.

[Exit Lady Capulet and Nurse]

Juliet: Goodbye. God knows when we will meet again. I have a feeling of fear which makes me cold and weak. Should I call them back? *[After a moment]* No, I have to do this on my own. Come on, bottle. *[She takes out the bottle Friar Laurence has given her]* *[Suddenly full of fear]* What if this mixture doesn't work? I'll have to get married tomorrow morning? No, no! *[Takes out her knife and puts it by her bed]* In that case, this knife will make sure that there is no marriage. *[Suddenly thinking of something else]* What if the Friar has given me poison? Perhaps he is afraid that this marriage will dishonour him, because he has already married me to Romeo. Yes, I am afraid it may be poison! *[Thinks for a moment]* No, no, it can't be poison. After all, he is a holy man. *[Suddenly full of fear again]* What if they put me in the tomb and I wake up before Romeo comes to get me? That's a frightening thought! No air can get into that tomb. I would not be able to breathe, and I would die before my Romeo comes.

Or if I do live . . . oh, the terror[78] of the place! A tomb where the dead bodies of my relatives have been lying for hundreds of years! A tomb where bloody Tybalt has been for only a few hours! Won't the horrible smells and terrible noises make me go mad? *[Frightened]* Oh, I think I see my dead cousin, looking for Romeo. Stop, Tybalt! Stop! Romeo, Romeo, Romeo, I drink to you! *[She drinks the mixture and falls down on her bed]*

Act 4, Scene 4

[Juliet's room. Juliet is lying on her bed. Enter Nurse]

Nurse: My lady! Juliet! She's fast asleep, I expect. Lamb! Lady! Bride[79]! Well, enjoy it while you can! *[Laughing]* Because I don't expect the Count Paris will let you rest very much tomorrow night! God forgive me! *[Juliet still doesn't move]* Oh, she is sleeping deeply. I must try and wake her up. Madam, madam! *[Comes closer]* Oh, she's all dressed. I must get her up. Lady! Lady! Lady! *[Touches Juliet, stands back shocked and then puts her ear against Juliet's heart]* Oh no! No! *[Screaming]* Help! Help! My lady's dead! Oh, bring me a strong drink! My lord! My lady!

[Enter Lady Capulet]

Lady Capulet: What's all this noise about?

Nurse: Oh terrible day!

Lady Capulet: What is the matter?

Nurse: *[Pointing at Juliet's body]* Look, look! Oh, heavy day!

Lady Capulet: *[Going up to Juliet and touching her body, then shaking her]* Oh my, Oh my! My child, my only life! Wake up, look up, or I will die with you. *[Running to the door]* Help! Help! Call for help!

[Enter Capulet]

Capulet: *[Not realizing what has happened]* Hurry up and get Juliet ready. Her lord is already here.

Nurse: *[Crying]* She's dead! She's dead! Oh terrible day!

Lady Capulet: *[Falling to the floor]* Terrible day! She's dead, she's dead, she's dead!

Capulet: *[Unable to believe them]* What? Let me see her! *[Goes to the bed and touches Juliet's face]* She's cold, her body is hard. Life has not touched these lips for a long time. Oh, death lies on her like a late frost[80] on the sweetest flower in the field.

Nurse: Oh terrible day!

Lady Capulet: Oh time of sorrow!

Capulet: *[Quietly]* Death has taken her away to make me cry out in sorrow. But now death has tied up my tongue and it won't let me speak.

[Enter Friar Laurence and Paris]

Friar Laurence: *[Pretending not to realize what has happened]* Come on, then. Is the bride ready to go to church?

Capulet: Ready to go, but never to return. *[to Paris]* Oh son, the night before your wedding day, Death has slept with your wife. Death is my daughter's husband, and when I die, I shall leave everything to him. Life, living, everything is Death's.

Capulet: *O son, the night before thy wedding-day*
Hath Death lain with thy wife. There she lies,
Flower as she was, deflowered by him.
Death is my son-in-law, Death is my heir.
My daughter he hath wedded. I will die,
And leave him all: life, living, all is Death's.

hath = has
thy = your
son-in-law = your daughter's husband
heir = the person that you give all your money to when you die

Paris: Have I waited so long to see this morning's face, only to see this sight?

Lady Capulet: Unhappy, hateful[81] day! I only had one, just one poor loving child. And cruel Death has taken her away.

Nurse: Most sorrowful day that I have ever known! Hateful day. There has never been a day as black as this!

Oh child, child! My child is dead, and with her die all my joys.

Paris: Oh hateful Death, you have taken away what was mine. Oh love! Oh life! Not life, but love in death!

Capulet: Oh terrible time, why did you come now to murder our celebrations? Oh child, child! My child is dead, and with her die all my joys.

Friar Laurence: *[Holding up his hands]* Peace now! All this crying will not put an end to this calamity. You shared this fair lady with heaven, and now heaven has her. And how much better for her that is! You wanted to make her as happy as possible. You hoped that this marriage would move her forward. So why are you crying, now that she has moved forward above the clouds and she is as high as heaven itself? Dry up your tears, and let us take her to church in her best clothes. Our feelings are weak and foolish. They make us full of sorrow for the one we love. But in our heads we know that we should feel glad for her.

Capulet: The musicians who had come for our celebrations will now play funeral[82] music. Our wedding dinner becomes a sad funeral dinner. And the flowers that were meant for a bride will lie upon her grave.

Friar Laurence: *[Taking Capulet, Lady Capulet and Paris out of Juliet's room]* In you go, sir, and madam. And you too, Count Paris. Get yourselves ready to follow this fair lady to her grave.

[Exit all]

Act 5, Scene 1

[In Mantua. Enter Romeo]

Romeo: If I can believe in the truth of sleep, my dreams tell me that there is some joyful news coming. My heart feels light, and all day I have been lifted up by cheerful thoughts. I dreamt that my lady came and found me dead. She breathed life back into me with her kisses. And when I came back to life, I was a king. *[Laughs]* Oh, how sweet love is, when even its dreams are so rich in joy.

[Enter Balthasar, Romeo's servant]

News from Verona! Greetings, Balthasar. Do you have any letters for me from the Friar? How is my lady? Is my father well? How is my Juliet? I ask you that again, because if she is well, then nothing can be wrong.

Balthasar: *[Quietly]* Then she is well and nothing can be wrong. Her body sleeps in the Capulets' tomb, and her spirit is living with the angels. I saw her being put into her grave, and I came straight here to tell you. Oh, I am so sorry to bring you this terrible news.

Romeo: *[Falling to his knees]* Is it really true? *[Looking up at the sky angrily]* The stars want to keep us apart. Well, you will not have what you want! *[to Balthasar]* Get me a pen and some paper, and find us some horses. I will leave this place tonight.

Balthasar: Please be strong, sir. You look pale, and I am worried that you may do something foolish.

Romeo: Nonsense. Now leave me alone, and do what I ask. You don't have any letters for me from the Friar?

Balthasar: No, my good lord.

Romeo: Never mind. Off you go. And get those horses. I'll join you very soon.

[Exit Balthasar]

Well, Juliet, I will lie with you tonight. Let me think how I can do it. *[Thinks for a moment]* Oh, troublesome thoughts are quick to enter the heads of desperate men. I remember that there's an apothecary who lives near here. I noticed him recently, he was out collecting plants. I'm sure that he will sell me some poison. Then I shall take it to Juliet's grave, and use it there.

[Exit Romeo]

Act 5, Scene 2

[At Friar Laurence's. Enter Friar John]

Friar John: Holy Friar, Brother, how are you!

[Enter Friar Laurence]

Friar Laurence: Friar John! Welcome from Mantua. What does Romeo say? Or do you have a letter for me from him?

Friar John: There is an infectious[83] illness here in the city at the moment. And I was stopped by some people who were checking houses for the illness. They thought I came from a house where the illness was. And so they shut me up there, and wouldn't let me out. And I wasn't able to go to Mantua.

Friar Laurence: *[Worried]* So who took my letter to Romeo, then?

Friar John: I could not send it – here it is, look! *[Holds up Friar Laurence's letter]* And I couldn't get a messenger to bring it back to you, because they were so afraid of the illness.

Friar Laurence: Unhappy fortune! It was not just a letter to a friend. It was full of very important news. And I am worried that if it hasn't reached Romeo, there may be great danger.

71

Friar John, go and get some tools and bring them here to my room.

Friar John: Brother, I'll go and bring them to you.

[Exit Friar John]

Friar Laurence: Now I must go to the tomb alone. Fair Juliet will wake in the next three hours. She will not be pleased that Romeo doesn't know what has happened. But I will write again to Mantua and she can stay at my room until Romeo comes. Poor Juliet, shut up in a dead man's tomb.

[Exit Friar Laurence]

Act 5, Scene 3

[At the churchyard[84]. Enter Romeo and Balthasar, carrying tools and a torch]

Romeo: Give me those tools and the torch. *[Balthasar hands them to Romeo]* Now, take this letter, and give it to my father early tomorrow morning. *[Romeo gives Balthasar a letter]* Go now, Balthasar. Whatever you hear or see, you must stay away. Don't try to stop me. If you come back, I swear that I will tear your body into pieces and cover the hungry churchyard with them.

Balthasar: I will go, sir. I won't cause you any trouble.

Romeo: You are a good friend. *[Gives Balthasar some money]* Take this. Good luck, and goodbye.

Balthasar: *[to himself]* I am going to hide near here and wait. I am worried about what he is going to do.

[Balthasar moves away]

Romeo: Hateful womb[85] of death! You have eaten the dearest thing on earth. And now I will push your mouth

72

open, and stuff you full with more food. *[Romeo opens the tomb]* This is not a grave. No, this is a room full of windows. For Juliet lies here. And her beauty fills it with light. *[Sees Juliet's body and goes to it]* Oh my love, my wife. Death may have taken away your sweet breath, but it has not taken away your beauty. I can still see beauty in the redness of your lips and cheeks. Pale Death has not covered you yet.

[Sees Tybalt's body lying next to Juliet] There lies Tybalt. What more can I do for you, but kill the hand that cut off your youth? Forgive me, cousin. *[Takes Juliet's hand]* Oh dear Juliet, why are you still so fair? Is Death keeping you here in the dark to be his lover? I will stay with you for ever in this house of night. Here will I stay, with the worms that are your maids[86]. My body is tired of life. I want to shake off the unlucky stars that hang around my neck. Eyes, look for the last time. Arms, hold your love for the last time! *[He takes Juliet in his arms]* And lips, you doors of breath, make your promise to Death. *[He takes out the bottle of poison]* Come, poison, take this tired little boat and throw it onto the rocks.

Here's to my love! *[He drinks the poison]* Oh apothecary, your poison works well. And so, with a kiss, I die. *[He kisses Juliet and then falls to the ground]*

[Enter Friar Laurence, with a light and tools. He sees Balthasar coming towards him in the darkness]

Friar Laurence: Who's there?

Balthasar: A friend who knows you well.

Friar Laurence: *[Recognizing Balthasar]* Peace be with you. Tell me, my good friend, is that a light I can see at the Capulets' tomb?

Balthasar: It is, holy sir. My master, Romeo, is there.

Friar Laurence: *[Worried]* Come with me to the tomb.

Balthasar: I cannot, sir. My master said that he would kill me if I watched what he was doing.

Friar Laurence: Stay then, I shall go alone. Suddenly I feel full of fear. I fear that something terrible may have happened. *[Calling out as he gets near to the tomb]* Romeo! *[Holds up his light and looks into the tomb]* Romeo! *[Sees Romeo lying next to Juliet, dead]* Oh, so pale! How has this terrible thing happened? *[Sees Juliet moving]* The lady is waking up.

Juliet: Oh Friar, where is my lord? I remember where I am supposed to be, and here I am. Where is my Romeo?

Friar Laurence: *[Hearing a noise]* I can hear something. Lady, leave this womb of death and unreal sleep. Something has gone terribly wrong with our plans. Come, come away. Your husband lies there dead. Come, we must go. Don't ask questions now, I can hear the nightwatchmen[87] coming. *[Juliet sits up and looks at Romeo, lying next to her]* Come, good Juliet. I cannot stay any longer.

Juliet: Go then, for I will not leave.

[Exit Friar Laurence]

What's this? A bottle in my true love's hand? *[She takes the bottle of poison from Romeo's hand and smells it]* Poison, I see, has brought him to his end. *[Holds the bottle up and sees that it is empty]* Oh, you have drunk it all, and not left a friendly drop to help me too. I will kiss your lips. Perhaps there is some poison left on them that will make me die. *[She kisses him]* Your lips are warm! *[She hears a noise]* Someone is coming! Then I shall be quick. *[Sees Romeo's knife and takes it out]* Oh happy knife, this is where you will stay now. *[Holds it against her heart]* Stay there, and let me die. *[Stabs herself and falls to the ground]*

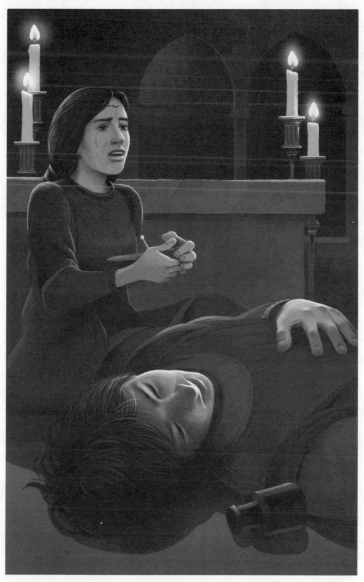

Oh happy knife, this is where you will stay now. Stay there,
and let me die.

[Enter night watchmen]

First watchman: What is this light? *[Sees Juliet's body]* Oh terrible sight! Here lies Juliet, bleeding[88], warm and newly dead. But she has been in this grave for two days. *[Calls out to the other watchmen]* Go and call the Prince! Run to the Capulets and the Montagues! And search the churchyard!

[Exit several night watchmen. They soon come back, with Balthasar and Friar Laurence]

Second watchman: Here is Romeo's servant. We found him in the churchyard.

Third watchman: And here is a friar, shaking and crying. He was coming out of the churchyard, with these tools.

First watchman: Don't let them go until the Prince arrives.

[Enter Prince Escalus, with servants]

Prince Escalus: What is going on, at this early hour? Why have we been woken?

[Enter Capulet and Lady Capulet, with servants]

Capulet: What is all the shouting about?

Lady Capulet: The people in the street were all crying 'Romeo' and 'Juliet', and running towards our tomb.

First watchman: *[to the Prince]* My lord, here lies Romeo, dead. And Juliet, who we thought was dead already. She is still warm, because she has just died.

Prince Escalus: Go and find out how these terrible things happened.

First watchman: Here is a friar, who had tools for opening a tomb, and Romeo's servant. We found them in the churchyard.

Capulet: *[Looking into the tomb]* Oh heavens! Oh wife, look how our daughter bleeds! She has that Montague's knife through her heart.

Lady Capulet: Oh my! What a sight.

[Enter Montague, with servants]

Prince Escalus: Come, Montague. You are up early to see your son cut down[89] early.

Montague: Oh my lord, my wife died last night. Her sorrow at my son's exile took her breath away. What other sadness can there be for me?

Prince Escalus: *[Taking his arm, and bringing him towards the tomb]* Look, and you will see.

Montague: *[Crying out]* Oh, this is not right! *[to Romeo]* How can you go to the grave before your father?

Prince Escalus: Try to be calm for a moment, and let us find out what happened here. *[to the night watchmen]* Bring forward the friar. *[Friar Laurence comes forward]*

Friar Laurence: Here I stand, to say that I have done wrong and to be forgiven.

Prince Escalus: Then tell us now what you know.

Friar Laurence: Romeo, who lies there dead, was Juliet's husband. And she, who lies there too, was Romeo's faithful wife. I married them on the day that Tybalt died. On that day, this new husband was exiled from the city. It was for him – not for Tybalt – that Juliet cried. *[He turns to the Capulets]* You wanted to marry her to Count Paris. So she came to me. She said she would kill herself if she could not be freed from this second marriage. So I gave her a sleeping mixture, which made people think she was dead. I wrote to Romeo. I asked him to come here tonight to take her from this tomb when she woke up. But my letter never arrived. So I came here alone tonight to take her back to my room while I sent for Romeo. But when I got here, just before she woke up, I found true Romeo dead. Juliet woke up, and I told her to come with me and be brave. But a noise scared me from the tomb and she wouldn't come with me. She was too desperate, and, it seems, she killed herself. This is all I know. If this has all gone wrong because of me, then take my old life.

Prince Escalus: *[Kindly]* You are a holy man. Where's Romeo's servant? *[Balthasar comes forward]* What can you tell us?

Balthasar: I brought my master the news that Juliet had died. And then he hurried here from Mantua. He gave me this letter for his father. *[Brings out the letter]* And he told me that he would kill me if I did not leave him alone at the tomb.

Prince Escalus: Give me the letter. *[Balthasar hands him the letter, and he reads it]* It seems that everything the Friar has told us is true. Romeo writes that he bought some poison from a poor apothecary and he came here to die and lie with Juliet. Where are these enemies? Capulet, Montague, see how your hate for each other has been punished. Love has killed your own children. And because I let this argument go on, I have lost my people too. We have all been punished.

Capulet: Oh, brother Montague, give me your hand. All I can ask you for is your hand in friendship.

Montague: *[Taking his hand]* But I shall give you more. I will put up a golden statue of your daughter. While Verona stands, nothing will be more precious than true and faithful Juliet.

Capulet: Romeo will be just as precious. I shall put a statue of him next to his lady. And they will stand there – Romeo and Juliet, who died because of our long argument.

Prince Escalus: Morning has brought with it a sad peace. The sun is too full of sorrow to shine. Go and we will talk more about these sad things. Some will be forgiven, and some will be punished. There has never been a sadder story than this story of Juliet and her Romeo.

Points for Understanding

Act 1

1 How did the Prince say he would punish the Capulets and Montagues if there was more fighting in the town?
2 Why was Romeo feeling so unhappy?
3 Why did Count Paris visit Capulet?
4 Why did Benvolio want Romeo to go to Capulet's party?
5 Who did Tybalt want to fight at the party, and why?
6 Why was Juliet shocked when Nurse told her who Romeo was?

Act 2

1 What did Juliet want Romeo to change about himself?
2 What did Romeo and Juliet decide to do?
3 Why was Friar Laurence worried about Romeo's plan?
4 Why did he decide to help him?
5 What message did Romeo give to Nurse for Juliet?
6 Why did Romeo want a rope ladder?

Act 3

1 Why didn't Romeo want to fight with Tybalt?
2 How did Mercutio die?
3 What was Romeo's punishment for killing Tybalt?
4 How did Romeo feel when he heard about his punishment, and why did he feel like this?
5 What did Lord Capulet do to try and stop Juliet thinking about her cousin's death?
6 What did Nurse tell Juliet to do?

Act 4

1 Who did Juliet meet at Friar Laurence's? What was he doing there?
2 Why did Juliet pick up a knife when she went to see Friar Laurence?
3 Friar Laurence gave Juliet a mixture. What will the mixture do?
4 What did Lord Capulet decide to do after Juliet came back from Friar Laurence's?
5 What four things was Juliet worried about before she drank the mixture?

Act 5

1 What news did Balthasar bring Romeo from Verona?
2 What did Romeo decide to do?
3 Why didn't Romeo get the letter that Friar Laurence sent to him?
4 What did Romeo do when he found Juliet inside the Capulets' tomb?
5 How did Juliet kill herself, and why?
6 What did Capulet and Montague decide to do at the end of the play?

Glossary

1 **playwright** (page 4)
   someone who writes plays, especially as their job.
2 **interval** (page 4)
   a short break between the parts of something such as a play or concert.
3 **performed** – *to perform* (page 5)
   act or sing in front of an audience.
4 **tomb** (page 7)
   a place or large stone structure where a dead person is buried.
5 **apothecary** (page 7)
   an old word for someone whose job was to prepare and sell medicines.
6 **servant** (page 11)
   someone whose job is to cook, clean, or do other work in someone else's home.
7 **sword** (page 11)
   a weapon with a short handle and a long sharp blade.
8 **stabs** – *to stab* (page 11)
   to push a knife or other sharp object into someone or something.
9 **villain** (page 11)
   an evil person or criminal.
10 **attendant** (page 12)
   someone whose job is to look after another person, especially someone with an important position or someone who is ill.
11 **enemy** (page 12)
   someone who is opposed to someone else and tries to harm them.
12 **punish** (page 12)
   to do something unpleasant to someone because they have done something bad or illegal.
13 **madam** (page 13)
   used as a polite way of talking to a woman who has an important social position.
14 **dawn** (page 13)
   the beginning of the day, when it begins to get light.
15 **sighing** – *to sigh* (page 13)
   to breathe out slowly making a long soft sound, especially because you are disappointed, tired, annoyed, or relaxed.

16 **dew** (page 13)

small drops of water that form on the ground at night.

17 **bud** (page 13)

a part of a plant that opens to form a leaf or flower.

18 **worm** (page 13)

a small creature with a long soft body and no bones or legs.

19 **cruel** (page 14)

making someone unhappy or upset.

20 **vow** (page 15)

a serious promise. **Chastity** is a way of life that does not include any sexual activity. Romeo is saying that the woman he loves has promised never to love or sleep with a man.

21 **honourable** (page 16)

if you are *honourable* you are morally good and deserving of respect.

22 **my lord** (page 16)

used as a polite way of talking to a man from the highest class of society.

23 **damage** (page 16)

to have a negative effect on someone or something.

24 **scornfully** (page 17)

if you are *scornful*, you feel that someone or something is not good enough to deserve your approval or respect. Romeo shows that he thinks Benvolio's advice is not helpful.

25 **master** (page 17)

a man who has control over servants, other people, or an animal.

26 **mask** (page 21)

something that you wear in order to hide part or all of your face.

27 **torch** (page 21)

a piece of wood with a flame at one end that is used as a light.

28 **jewel** (page 22)

a hard valuable stone that has been cut and polished.

29 **precious** (page 22)

very valuable.

30 **dove** (page 22)

a white bird. Doves are often used as a sign of peace.

31 **crow** (page 22)

a large ugly black bird that makes a loud sound.

32 **how dare?** (page 22)

if you say *how dare you/she/it etc.* you are shocked and angry about something that someone has done or said.